A Clean Heart

& Spare Parts

*A Journey Through Breast Cancer
. . . the Journey Continues*

BOB & KRISTI ARMSTRONG

For Additional Copies Contact
Kristi Armstrong at

www.kristiarmstrong.com

A Clean Heart and Spare Parts

Copyright © 2007 by Bob and Kristi Armstrong

Third Printing 2010

ISBN: 0-935515-76-3

Published by:
EVANGEL PUBLICATIONS
129 Kingswood Drive
Huntsville, Alabama 35806

Scripture quotations are from the New King James Version of the Bible unless otherwise stated.

Printed in the United States of America

Contents

Acknowledgements

Bob and I wish to express our gratitude to our family, our church and other friends for their support during our journey through cancer.

Credit for the cover design is given to Joel Franks with Windward Media, Inc. of Savannah, Tennessee. Joel, we are grateful for your contribution to the book.

Rhonda Lackey, with In His Image Photography of Savannah, Tennessee, supplied the picture for the back cover and arranged the other pictures in the book. Thank you, Rhonda, for your help.

- Bob & Kristi Armstrong

Foreword

Kristi Armstrong lights up the room and brightens her corner of the world. Wherever she goes she spreads cheer. Her radiant smile radically alters the atmosphere of any group into which she enters. She is one of the most positive people I've ever known.

Kristi is a woman of deep and abiding faith. She is fanatically in love with the Lord Jesus Christ and dares to believe that He is literally "in charge" in this universe and in our daily lives. All who know her are in love with her and are inspired by her.

Cancer challenged her and lost. Those of us who witnessed her journey from the discovery of her malignancy, through the times of treatment, to the ringing of the bell on victory day...right up to today...are in awe of her. Her inner-glory as a Christian has shown in her countenance and in her behavior as long as I have known her and it has never glowed more gloriously than during her successful battle with cancer.

Kristi is madly in love with her husband, Bob. They are a "pattern" for couples to follow. After years of marriage they still look "googoo" eyed at each other. Theirs is a world class love story. Their romance is on fire with true love as God intended for every married couple.

Bob has been Kristi's partner in this recent battle as he has been throughout their marriage. He has prayed for her, chauffeured her, encouraged her, loved and supported her, and admired her through this entire episode. Her sons, Zack and Luke, her daughter-in-law, Kristina, and her grandson, Tyler, have all been there for her.

Any person who is facing cancer or any other threatening disease will be greatly encouraged and enlightened by reading and re-reading this book. Those whose friends or loved ones are facing these health issues, will also profit greatly from this "delightful read."

Read this book and bask in the "Son" shine of this courageous Christian woman. She is intelligent, Spirit-filled, honest, and hilariously funny. I predict that you will laugh a lot, cry a little, and be grateful for the rest of your life.

Kristi's Pastor,
Dr. Jerry L. Spencer

Be anxious for nothing, but in everything by prayer and supplication, with thanksgiving, let your requests be made known unto God; and the peace of God, which surpasses all understanding, will guard your hearts and minds through Christ Jesus.

(Philippians 4:6-7)

Chapter One

I've Got What?

In the summer of 2005, I was a healthy thirty-seven year old woman, happily married to my husband, Bob, with two sons and a wonderful family. Life was good. By the fall of that same year, I was a thirty-seven year old woman, happily married to my husband, Bob, with two sons, a wonderful family, and cancer. Not exactly the "family addition" we had planned.

To start at the beginning, I'll go back to January of 2004 when I underwent shoulder surgery. During the process, I had a mammogram because of pain across my chest. The left side was abnormal, but because of my age and a normal ultrasound, there seemed to be no reason for concern. Time progressed and a small lump became noticeable in the upper inner quadrant of my left breast. I had it checked a few times during the year of 2004, but nothing seemed amiss. By the summer of 2005, the mass was very distinct and painful to the touch. I called my gynecologist and scheduled a visit in October.

As I made the appointment, I reassured myself that it was just a previously torn muscle from my past shoulder injury. During the appointment, the doctor took me very seriously because she had recently lost her grandmother to breast cancer. She ordered a mammogram to be done as soon as possible. During the week of waiting for the test, I lost my precious ninety-two year old grandfather. He passed away on October 30th. On November 1st, I went in for a mammogram and ultrasound. The next day, one hour before my grandfather's funeral, the doctor called with the results

— suspicion of carcinoma, CANCER! [A note about my Paw-Paw. He was a World War II Veteran, so he was given a full military funeral. It was a beautiful November day with a cloudless clear blue sky. I named it a Paw-Paw day. Remember that for later. It is important when we discuss chemotherapy.]

Bob and I chose to keep the information between the two of us until after the burial. We had planned to wait until that evening to share the news with my parents, Lonnie and Bonnie Godwin. Mom, Grand Maw Pearl, Bob, and I were viewing the grave when Mom's cell phone rang in her van. I answered the call from my dad. He asked if I was alright, considering the funeral circumstances, but his question was my undoing. To his surprise, I told him about the phone call from the tests. He assured me that all was well and that God was in control. Hanging up, it was then time to look my sweet mom in the eye and tell her of our concerns. What a way to end the day of burying your father. A child, possibly with cancer, would rock any mother's faith. But Mom took everything in stride and confirmed what Dad had said. God was in control.

You have to know that my husband and family are devout Christians. We believe in the miracle working power of God. We began to pray as we awaited the appointment with the breast disease specialist on November 8th in Memphis, Tennessee. I was referred to him by my doctor, but God directed my path. Bob and I went to the appointment not really knowing what to expect. The doctor did an ultrasound to check the mass. He decided to do a needle core biopsy to sample the tissues. Now, time out! What was I feeling? Totally numb. I have always faced hard times with humor, but this time I was speechless. The doctor usually did that type of biopsy on a Friday. This was Tuesday and his schedule was loaded. God gives us favor in man's eyes when we place our trust in Him. The doctor decided to do the biopsy that evening and promised to call with the results on Thursday.

As the procedure began, Bob intended to be involved and to watch as the doctor removed the tissue samples, but that didn't work. He decided the chair against the wall looked really comfortable, so he took a seat. The procedure went really well with very little discomfort. As the samples were removed, the doctor told us that the tissue did not look good. What did that mean? I can't have cancer. I'm healthy. Life was good. Bob and I started home, still trusting that God was in control. We knew that the people at our home church, Sharon Baptist, were praying and were believing for a good report.

On Thursday morning, I was on my way for a haircut when my cell phone rang. I looked at the area code 901. The call was from Memphis, probably my doctor. I was near my brother's business, so I pulled in the parking lot and answered the call. My surgeon had called from a seminar in Atlanta, Georgia to speak to me personally. He said, "I'm sorry. It is cancer." Patrick had just opened the van door when I finished the call. I told him, "I have cancer, Patrick." He answered, " Everything will be okay. God is in control." I called Bob to tell him the results. My husband and family live what they believe and know that nothing takes God by surprise. He said, "Alright, God is bigger than cancer. Do you want me to come and get you?" I said, "No." He then proceeded to tell me that he was so excited about the things that God could do through this. To be honest, he almost hurt my feelings. Sure, he had the right attitude, but breast cancer was going to be hard. Anyway, I told him that I really needed a haircut. God's peace overflowed my soul and body as I headed to Selmer for a new style.

Here's a note — if you have cancer or are diagnosed with a life-threatening disease, don't let it rule your life. You are still the same person. You still have the same favorite color. You still hate liver. "Trust in the Lord with all your heart, and lean not on your own understanding," Proverbs 3:5. Know that this struggle is in your life for a reason and although you may not understand it, you can be strong through it.

The day after I received the phone call that altered my life, Bob had to be away on business. He offered to cancel the meeting, but didn't because I needed some time alone to sort things out in my mind. Well, my mom was determined to help me "sort things." She came to the house, armed with books, videos, and scriptures to help build my faith for the fight ahead. We watched a video of a cancer survivor's miraculous testimony. During the talk, the lady shared a scripture that I adopted and applied to my life that day. It was Psalm 118:17: "I shall not die, but live, and declare the works of the Lord." The lady was standing before a packed audience as she told of her life-threatening struggle against cancer, how God had sustained her through the treatments, and of her resolve to share her story with anyone willing to listen. I took her example as my role model. I wanted to allow God to use me and breast cancer for His glory.

There is never a good time to be sick, especially with cancer, but in my heart I felt that I was on a specific time table set by God. He has a loving way of placing us in circumstances that are beyond our capabilities that His character may be revealed to us. I appeared to be a healthy, thirty-seven year old woman, but I had a silent killer in my left breast.

_Chapter Two_____

What Now?

Educate, learn, ask questions, talk to other survivors. After I was diagnosed with breast cancer, my mind went in a thousand directions all at once. I knew that I had to take charge of my life and of the turmoil that was facing me. I first consulted the word of God, where I was reminded that our life is in His hands. Isaiah 49:16 states that we are inscribed in the palm of His hand. God knows our days. He is our Creator. We must put total trust in His sovereignty and in His will for our lives. If you have an illness or are facing a hardship, rest in this truth.

The Monday after my cancer was confirmed, Bob, our younger son Zack, Mom, Dad, and I made the trip to Memphis to learn more about the type of cancer I had. This was on November 14, 2005. The surgeon was very informative and we flooded him with questions. He taped our consultation so that we could refer to the information later. During an appointment of this magnitude, facts are sometimes blurred by emotions and stress. Having the tape was helpful for later when questions arose. From the visit, a November 28th surgery date was scheduled for a lumpectomy of the left breast.

As a closing comment, we were offered an MRI of both breasts to see if there were any other problems that needed attention. We opted to have the scan, so it was scheduled for November 17th. A call came on November 22nd that two more suspicious areas needed biopsies. I began to keep a journal which I kept throughout my cancer journey.

The entry for this day was:

The MRI results show that there may be two more tumors. Tomorrow, Bob and I have to go to Memphis for another ultrasound and for more biopsies. How do I feel? Tired. This week, waiting on surgery has drained me. Lord, please keep the surgery date for November 28th.

Psalm 16:7-9, "I will bless the Lord who has given me counsel; my heart also instructs me in the night seasons. I have set the Lord always before me; because He is at my right hand I shall not be moved. Therefore my heart is glad, and my glory rejoices; My flesh also will rest in hope."

The next day turned into an eight hour ordeal of mammograms, ultrasounds, and twelve biopsies. The diagnostic doctor was trying to get sufficient tissue for clear lab results. I thank God for the doctors and medical personnel that He placed in our path. The next day was Thanksgiving day. What a way to get out of cooking for the big family meal! On Saturday morning, November 26, two days before the scheduled lumpectomy, the Women's Clinic phoned. "We have to step back and regroup. Two other spots have shown cancer activity. You will not have surgery on Monday. Your surgeon will be calling you."

Okay, we need a recap. My cancer diagnosis came on November 10. The surgery date that had been set was now canceled. Other circumstances with scheduling arose, such as getting a plastic surgeon involved in the surgical process. A new surgery date was set for December 21, 2005, four days before Christmas. Well, Thanksgiving had been interrupted, why not Christmas?

The pressure of getting the tumor out of my body was beginning to build. Friends and family began to question if we needed to find a different, more aggressive plan of action. The doctors assured us that the cancer did not form overnight, and that another few days would not make a big difference. But it did to us. Just knowing that the cancer was there caused a lot of stress. We just wanted it out.

During this time, God taught me many things. Blind faith and trusting Him completely were two major lessons. My Sunday school teacher and close friend, Kristy Guyer, taught me a very deep truth without even realizing it at the time. Her lesson was on one subject, but as a side note, she mentioned John 4:4: "But He (Jesus) needed to go through Samaria." The scripture is talking about the woman at the well, but it meant something totally different to me. Jesus did not have to go through Samaria on the journey, but He needed to. I did not have to have cancer, but I needed to. God's plan is much higher than ours. His thoughts are higher than our thoughts. Each of us has a journey that we need to take. How we walk the road is our choice. Detours in life can be viewed as inconveniences, a disturbance in our peaceful life, or as an opportunity for God to use us to help others. Bob and I spent numerous hours in doctor's office waiting rooms during the first few months after my diagnosis. Instead of feeling sorry for ourselves, we tried to make the best of the situation. Bob would walk around the clinic introducing himself to patients and their families. He would get their addresses and send cards of encouragement. I would compare stories with fellow patients and share scriptures that God had given us to keep our faith strong. We could have missed countless opportunities for people to bless us and for us to be a blessing if we had been consumed with our own fears. God has a purpose for every place life sends you. Take the time to find the reasons.

I recorded this in my journal on December the 2nd:

My dad called today. He shared with me that cancer is the vehicle to take me where God wants me. When I arrive, there will no longer be a need for cancer. Kristy Guyer's quoting of John 4:4 confirms that it was needed for

Jesus to go through Samaria. It is needed for me to go through cancer.

My friend and Sunday School class encourager, Sherrie Gray, called today. She said, "Maybe God will have you write a book with faith and humor."

And now, I have tried. One thing that comes to mind at this point on dealing with a cancer diagnosis is one's own mortality. In years past, a cancer diagnosis was a death sentence. Due to tireless research by the medical community, there is hope. Even with this, our lives are in God's hands. The sovereignty of God is sometimes difficult to grasp, but He does know best. The first thing you must do is make sure that you belong to Him. Romans 10:9-13 states that "For whoever calls on the name of the Lord shall be saved." That is the most important step in facing cancer, peace with Jehovah God. Next is to surrender to God's plan. The thought of leaving this life at an early age is frightening. Fear of the unknown is a major hurdle. Psalm 23:4 says "Yea, though I walk through the valley of the shadow of death, I will fear no evil; for You are with me." Notice the passage said through. I remember a sermon by Reverend Billy Graham when explaining death; he used the illustration of standing on the side of a highway and a semi-truck passing. The shadow of the truck would hit you. That is a good example of death for a believer, being hit by the shadow. For a non-believer, it is as if they were hit by the truck. Reading about Heaven I have learned that it is a wonderful place with beauty beyond compare. The only sadness is for those left behind. The void left by a departed loved one is tough to bear. There again, "Let the peace of God rule in your hearts," Colossians 3:15. My pastor, Dr. Jerry Spencer, says this when he talks about Heaven, "Heads, I win! Tails, I win!"

We have the Bible as an instruction guide. Use the word of God and trust in the sovereignty of God. Psalm 34:19 states, "Many are the afflictions of the righteous,

but the Lord delivers him out of them all."
My dad has written quite a few songs over
the past twenty years. One of my favorites
is *Living in Him.* The chorus reads:

"I am the man who's entered Beulah
land.
Fountains are flowing free,
meeting my every need.
Peace and contentment mine.
His presence so divine.
Loving Him all the time.
Living in Him."

As December 21st approached, everything became very focused. Bob and I
asked for family and friends to come by
the house and have special prayer with us.
We felt that it was important to keep information clear for the people we love. I
have heard of the calm in the eye of a
storm and there was no doubt that we
were there. Cancer hit just like a tornado
with things flying around, chaos every-
where, and blinding confusion. Outside, in

our world, things seemed to be falling apart, but we were peacefully watching the drama unfold. Total surrender to God's plan is a very settling choice. "He leads me in the paths of righteousness for His name's sake," Psalm 23:3. We are walking this path for God's reputation, not ours.

Our caravan left for Memphis at about 4:30 am. I can honestly tell you that I was really not stressed. Dad and Mom called to check and see that we were up. They wanted to make sure that I was alright. I told them that I needed to get to Memphis to "get something off my chest." That's right! Actual humor in the face of cancer surgery.

I was taken in for surgery at around 2:00pm and got back to the room by 6:00 pm. The night was a little rough due to the affect of the anesthesia. By 7:00am, I was up with my hair combed and make-up in place. The entire time, I refused to give in to the thought of not winning this battle with cancer.

While I was in surgery, there was a

waiting room full of family and friends. According to Bob, it was not a somber atmosphere. They feared being asked to leave because of all the laughter and noise. I was glad for all the encouragement. They came into my little pre-surgery room, two at a time, to talk and pray with me. I had left a book, a type of journal, in the waiting room for visitors to write me a note. I like to know what is going on, so this gave me insight for the hours that I was "under." It is now my precious possession. Sometimes, I get it out and read the wonderful thoughts and prayers that were lifted for me that day.

Before the mastectomy, I made an appointment to meet my oncologist. I wanted to meet him and let him see who I was. I told him that if I was different after the surgery, to please help me. Everything went well, so we set up a surgery time to have a port implanted. That was accomplished on January 16th and we started chemotherapy the next day. Bob and I got to the clinic at 10:00am and the process began. We were sitting in the waiting room, waiting for Armstrong to be called. I did not mean to make Bob sad, but I just looked at him and asked, "Am I going to be okay?" He started to cry. Through everything, to this point, Bob and I had only cried once. At that moment, I realized the stress that my husband was carrying. He knew that I would be just fine. It was just the fact that I was having to go through pain and suffering. He wanted to take the chemo for me, but I had to do it. Even to this day, if I ever hesitate or have a concerned look in my eyes, he says, "You're a healed woman!"

On January 23 I wrote:

January 17th was the first chemo. I had a port put in the day before and had a MUGA heart test the morning of my first treatment.

While Bob and I waited for four hours for the treatment, we talked in a small library at the West Clinic. I made a statement about death and Bob started to cry, and I cried. It was very stressful.

We had just dried our tears when Cindy Inman, my chemo nurse, brought by an envelope and said, "Hi." The note had a printout of the words of "When I Call On Jesus", a solo I do at church. Her note read- I know you have the words memorized, but sometimes it helps to read and meditate.

Cindy's act of kindness helped us through an emotional moment. Thinking back, our sons, Luke and Zack, stayed strong through the entire ordeal, as well. If they shed any tears, I am not aware of it. Luke even offered to shave his head in a show of support. Privately, they each asked me if I was going to be alright. They wanted to know if I was going to beat this. I told each of them that with God's help, I would be just fine. I love them for their strength and support. I actually missed Luke and Kristina's wedding on December 27, 2005. I was dehydrated and still sore from my surgery. Life goes on even if you are fighting cancer. Don't allow bitterness to creep in and steal your joy. You must be the center of your attention. Getting better needs to be the focus of your energy. Starting on January 17, 2006, surviving chemotherapy was my goal. The next fifteen months were defined by my getting a treatment every three weeks.

I shared earlier that in my heart I felt that I was on God's timetable. That proved to be true in one obvious way when our church choir was scheduled to record a live DVD on January 13, 2006. But wait a minute, I had a mastectomy on December 21st and was due to start chemotherapy on January 17th. I wanted to be a part of the recording because I love to sing, especially with Sharon Baptist Celebration Choir. We are more of a family than a loft full of singers. I received endless prayer and support from my fellow choir members. I was the soloist for the song "When I Call On Jesus" by Nicole C. Mullin and it was on the schedule of songs for the recording. What an honor to stand that night and sing with all my might that all things are possible when you call on Jesus. I wasn't just singing it, I was living it! At that time I learned that God will show Himself strong if we will become available for His purpose. Bob and I had the privilege of sharing our personal testimony just before my special.

There is a little story of how Bob and I met. In July of 1997, I worked at a dental office and Bob was a patient there. He had just been down-sized from a twenty-five year career in paper mills. His dental insurance was to expire in a few months, so he came in for a check-up. I really liked him, but he thought I was just being kind to a guy who had lost his job. Because of our age difference, he did not feel comfortable asking me for a date. Due to my planning, he had to endure shots in the mouth at two different appointments. You see, the two teeth that needed work were in the same quadrant, so they could have been done on the same visit. But I thought that he needed a little more encouragement to know that I was interested in him, so I booked separate appointments. The next week on July 24th, he brought me a birthday present. I knew then that he loved me, so I called and asked him for a date. I even offered to pay for it. He had just lost his job! Isn't that funny? Me, living with my parents, offering to pay his way to a movie. Bob figured out then that I was kind of silly, but he loves me anyway. We were married on March 14, 1998. God knew that day that we would face cancer together. I am so thankful that He gave me Bob for the journey.

Chapter Three

Bob's Perspective
HEY, THIS AFFECTS ME, TOO!

Kristi is a few years younger than me (actually it is several years) and she has always told me she would take care of me in my older days. Breast cancer just did not seem to fit into our plans. She is the godly wife I had prayed for over a span of many years. We had gotten to know each other just after I had been downsized from a 25-year career. The reason I throw that in is that I felt the same peace after her diagnosis that I felt after I lost my job, and that situation has turned out to be terrific. I have since gone to work for a company which was founded 117 years ago and is based on solid moral principles. My manager and most of my co-workers are Christians. When we received the cancer diagnosis, people all over the country within my company began praying for and encouraging us.

God's peace is sort of a strange thing which could be spooky if you didn't know where it was coming from. Throughout my life, I have made my share of boneheaded decisions. Even some of the prayers I have prayed were not very smart. Fortunately, God knows best. In the last few years, I have learned to pray more for His will instead of my wants. I finally realized that His timetable did not necessarily agree with mine and in the long run, He will always do what's best. We prayed for His will before Kristi's diagnosis, but we did ask Him to make the tests negative, "if it was His will." We prayed the same way after the "C" word was confirmed. Thankfully, His peace sustained me and allowed me to encourage Kristi through some rough times.

Kristi has a wonderful outgoing personality and she is tough. She has felt absolutely horrible at times and I was the only one who had any idea of how bad she really felt. I'm sure she often kept much of the worst parts from me. I feel we communicate really well when compared to most couples. I strongly urge both the patient and the loved ones to let each other know what is going on between the ears. If you need a cool rag on your head and a place to sit when the nausea is being relieved, let the caregiver know. Caregiver, ask questions, make suggestions, then listen.

Throughout most of the treatments, Kristi could not do any shopping alone. There wasn't a problem with her, but she would inevitably encounter some less than encouraging stories. I realize that people must sometimes share their pain to help them cope. We just had to work through some of the stories of losing a loved one. You view that differently when you are in the midst of cancer treatments.

I fell in love with Kristi, not just body parts. Just because her shape was altered a little did not change my love for her. Shucks, my shape has changed since we married and she still loves me. Why should I do any less for her? She seemed a little apprehensive before she first showed me the surgery site. I did not have much of an idea of what to expect, but I knew the surgeon did an excellent job. He made a small horizontal incision and used drawstring sutures. The stitches were sticking out approximately one quarter inch along the incision. She mustered the courage to look closely at herself from the waist up. As she was looking in the mirror, she called me in to see what I thought. When she turned around, the first thing that came to my mind and out of my mouth was: "Let me get a marker and draw a nose and smile on your stomach and your chest will look like it's winking at me." Can you get the visual? Anyway, from that point on Kristi seemed to be a little more at ease.

With surgery out of the way, chemo was the next step on our journey. We were certain her hair would be going soon. Shortly after the first "Red Devil," Tootsie had her hair cut very short. When it actually started falling out, she had it buzzed. Haley, her hairdresser, is a friend as well as a fellow choir member. Haley cried while Kristi and I laughed. (I have been follically-challenged as long as Kristi has known me and it seemed a little ironic that she would have less hair than me for awhile.) Anyway, Kristi and I came home with her hair about a millimeter long. The idea was good on the surface. There would not be hair falling out all over the house, in the bed, etc. However, we did not think of one thing. The stubble was very prickly. It was like little needles sticking in her scalp each time she wore her wig or night cap. We needed help. The solution?—duct tape. How you might ask? Well, we took strips of the duct tape and wrapped it over her head. It is incredible how many of the little giblets of hair each strip pulled out. We were able to get about 95 percent of the stubble before her head got too sensitive to continue. Kristi called it her "Redneck waxing".

For the next several months my Tootsie wore a wig. It looked good, but was not the most comfortable thing to wear. One of the most interesting stories regarding the wig happened on one of her singing trips. The trio she sings with, Allen Guyer and Triumph, was invited to Monette, Arkansas to sing. Monette is a thriving metropolis (about the size of Savannah, Tennessee) three hours north of Memphis. The audience was a group of wonderful people who loved their music. At the end, the trio lined up to meet and greet the crowd. One particular sweet lady came up to Kristi and was extremely complimentary. She said, "I love your voice, you are so pretty, and I just love your hair. I would give anything if I could get my hair to look like yours." Do you know where this is going? Yep, Kristi shucked off the wig and held it out to the lady. The poor lady's mouth dropped open and she walked off with a dazed look on her face. How many times do we do this with God? We pray and pray for a particular need and when He says, "Okay, here it is!", we walk away without receiving it. Do we question His ability to provide the things we ask for? Do we question His willingness to give us the desires of our heart? Do we really want what we are asking for? Whatever the reason, we often fail to accept God's provision. We should take our own prayers seriously. God does.

Kristi has accused me of being a little too optimistic at times. I have noticed over the years that regardless of the circumstances, God can make something positive out of them. I will relate a couple of examples. Tootsie had finished the "Red Devil" and had just taken her first Taxol/-Herceptin treatment. Each variation of the chemo has its own set of side effects. Apparently, these chemicals affect the ability of the body to handle stressful situations. Anyway, we were having a typical March afternoon, a little windy. Well, it was very windy with tornado alarms sounding. My dear ninety-two year old mother, Mama Cile, and one of my brothers had just driven behind our house to come inside the basement. Within seconds, a straight line wind blew a huge hickory tree across our house. As a note of optimism, Mother and Sammy could have dropped by five seconds later, but they didn't. They had just crossed the path of the tree and were not harmed.

The tree crushed my work truck and the roof was touching the middle of the seat. We thought of marketing this truck to fathers of dating age daughters. There would be no worry about the couple sitting too close. Another note of optimism: the truck cushioned the blow of the tree so there was not any serious structural damage to the south side of the house. However, one third of the deck was on the ground and rain was coming through the den ceiling.

Do you remember the comment about the chemo affecting the ability to handle stress? Well, all of the excitement got Kristi into a bad shape. She almost fainted, was struggling to breathe, and her lips started to turn blue. Some of our family and church family had already started responding to the news of the tree on the house. Folks had come over to pray with us and to do whatever we needed. Isn't God's family great?

Fortunately, one of our friends who came by was a registered nurse, Donna Norris. She went into Doctor Mode and started assessing Kristi's condition. She called our oncology nurse, Cindy Inman, who gave instructions to get Tootsie back to normal. There is no doubt that God directed us to the doctor who had Cindy as his nurse.

Kristi and I complement each other very well. We tend to fill in the gaps of each other's lives. One of my shortcomings is my selective memory. That can actually be a good thing when it comes to forgetting some of the rough times in life. Not long ago, I commented to Kristi that I had been so blessed that nothing really bad had ever happened to me. You know, she reminded me of several instances when I really did have some trying times. Fortunately, God sustained me through all of them and allowed the bad memories to fade.

We recently heard a minister preach on Luke 22:31-32. It reads: "And the Lord said, Simon, Simon! Indeed, Satan has asked for you, that he may sift you as wheat. But I have prayed for you, that your faith should not fail; and when you have returned to Me, strengthen your brethren." I am not implying that our trials could come close to what Peter faced, but in our eyes we have felt "sifted." It is an amazing comfort to know that Jesus loves us enough to pray for our faith not to fail. Our prayer is that this recording of our journey will "strengthen" our brothers and sisters.

We have been overwhelmed by love

and support from our family, friends, and extended family. I had three pretty good cries through our ordeal. The first was just after the diagnosis. Even though I had a peace about it all, I didn't like the thought of all Kristi would be going through. The second cry came just before her first "Red Devil" or "Big Red" hook-up. Kristi asked me, "Are you going to be okay if I'm not?" I told her that she was going to be fine. She asked me again and I replied the same way. When she asked me the third time if I was really sure, I lost it. Even though I knew she would be alright, for a split second I considered the possibilities and I broke down. The third time was tears of joy. After the last of twenty IV treatments, we were allowed to ring the bell at the clinic signifying that chemo was over. After fifteen months, it was finally finished! We both shed tears of joy while hugging each other. We have shed a few more tears over the outpouring of love and concern from our friends.

Kristi's particular variety of breast cancer was hormone driven. Because of this, her hormones had to be reduced. The chemo treatments took care of this, but she had three weeks between them to replenish. After the chemo, Tamoxifen was prescribed to be taken each day for five years. This stuff blocks estrogen daily. In the normal course of aging, the hormone reduction is a process which takes years to accomplish. Instead of years to get accustomed to the changes, we had a few days or weeks. The hot flashes have been amazing. I am surprised I haven't come down with pneumonia. Sometimes I come home to a normal temperature and sometimes it seems like a meat locker. Other than the obvious discomfort, these flashes have caused Kristi a few other difficulties, such as make-up application. Some mornings it melts off her face before she gets it applied. It is not uncommon for her to wake up in the middle of the night drenched in sweat. This, of course, prevents the good REM sleep. By the way, I miss out on the

REM sleep every now and then, too. But, as we have said before, it is our journey through breast cancer. An oscillating fan has proved to be a wonderful investment.

I am blessed that Tootsie is not a moody person. However, there have been some minor challenges due to the hormone thing. As I mentioned before, communication is one of the prime keys to successfully get through breast cancer. Each spouse must share feelings, insecurities, fears, doubts, etc. Major changes have been taking place and you must let each other know what you think and feel. A feeling that may appear to be very important or pressing today may or may not be there tomorrow. Deal with each set of emotions individually.

This wraps up my little chapter. I hope it helps. You can get through these tough situations. Trust the Lord, maintain a sense of humor, and take care of business one day at a time.

I shall not die, but live, And declare the works of the Lord.

(Psalm 118:17

Hair Today, Gone Tomorrow!

You lose a lot going through chemo-therapy. After the first treatment, I did really well. I told a few people, "Let everything within me, even chemo, bless His holy name." Shortly after the second treatment, my hair started falling out so one of my nurses suggested that it might be a good idea to shave my head. Bob went with me to see Haley Surratt. We told her to buzz it. She wanted to know if we were really sure. It was pretty neat because she was the one to cut my hair on the day I got the news of my diagnosis. Now here she was, shaving my head. I was really proud of my bald head, but it did look different. What a great way to try out new styles! Start with nothing and grow through different looks. I was actually bald, I mean totally slick, for at least six months. I took that time to try out different variations of scarves, hats, and wigs. I was known for just pulling my wig off if it got too hot or uncomfortable. Bob has shared one of the stories in his chapter. When you go through cancer, appearance sort of takes a back seat. You see life and living through different eyes. Let your trials make you, not break you.

I entered this in my journal on February 7, 2006-

This morning I felt depressed. Yesterday, I had no strength and I slept a lot. I choose to get up at 8:00am and straighten the house and start laundry. I prayed to God this morning- I feel like Moses when he left Egypt, wandering in the desert. I need to find a burning bush. I found it! Thank you God for hearing me:

John 14:27: "Peace I leave with you, My peace I give to you; not as the world gives do

I give to you. Let not your heart be troubled, neither let it be afraid."

John 14:1: "Let not your heart be troubled..." "Let" is a permissive word. It means to allow. God tells us in John 14 to not LET our hearts be troubled.

This revelation has carried us through a lot of difficult days. The effects of chemotherapy is cumulative, therefore, it gets harder as you go. My treatment regimen included three rounds of what is nicknamed the "Red Devil." Rightly named. With these three, all hair was gone, I had extreme fatigue, and I found it difficult to eat. Here are a few things I learned during these treatments that made them more tolerable. Carry a jacket or blanket to the clinic because most people get really cold during the infusion. Never eat something you really enjoy during treatment. I still have not touched some of the things I ate on those days. A bag of sour candy or lemon drops were nice to have to help neutralize the metal taste in my mouth.

White grape juice was a smooth drink that seemed to go down easy. Drink plenty of water. The medicine will do its job, but it is your responsibility to flush it out. We learned many of these tips from other patients at the clinic. My first six treatments lasted for about five and a half hours, so be prepared to take a nap or read a book. That was a long time to sit hooked up to an IV pole. The night after treatment, I would set an alarm clock for every two hours. I felt it necessary to drink plenty of water and go to the bathroom. My body was being bombarded by chemicals. I needed to do everything I could to help it. This was a battle.

February 19, 2006:

I haven't written for awhile. The 3rd treatment was really bad. It will be a week ago tomorrow and I haven't bounced back yet. I feel tired, my body smells like chemicals, my nose bleeds, and my throat has sores. Just the thought of walking into that clinic makes me want to throw up.

I am sharing my journal because I want to help people who face cancer treatment. It is a difficult road to walk, but it can be done. I am living proof. The chemo is killing cells, both good and bad. I have shared with others that after those first infusions, I felt I was as close to death as I ever could be without actually dying. I experienced a sinking feeling inside. I knew that the chemo was working really well, maybe too well. During that dark day, February 19th, I told Bob that he must help me find something that I could eat without getting sick. My sister-in-law, Una Armstrong, came over and tried to get me to drink something. She mixed a little coke and sugar. I was able to swallow the little mixture and in a few hours, I was able to eat a sandwich. On a different occasion, my mom gave me a dill pickle slice to hold in my mouth. During the treatments, I experienced a nasty metallic taste. The dill pickle would change that bad taste so that I could try some food. Eating with a plastic spoon made a difference to me. I guess because my mouth already had the taste of metal, plastic was the way to go. I would eat yogurt morning and night to help my digestive system. Nothing smelled right or tasted normal. My most used phrase was, "What is that smell?" My senses seemed to be heightened. I learned a lot about myself at that time, things I never would have known had I not gone through the treatments. It almost made it worth the trouble.

My journal entry was:

On Wednesday morning I went to Corinth to get my white blood cell booster shot. By Thursday, the worst day of my life, I was in an awful shape. Four times I asked Bob to shoot me. I got sick a couple of times and my bones and skin hurt. I felt like an orange that had been totally peeled down. Nothing left but the seeds. The word of God is referred to as seed in Mark 4. I found Psalm 107:20- "He sent His word and healed them and delivered them from their destructions." When nothing else was left of me, I found HIM.

Looking back, God took me from that day and rebuilt me from that low state. I would not take anything for that time. I felt so close to my Heavenly Father that I could almost hear His heart beating. Jesus was a man who knew about suffering. If He could die on a rugged cross for me, He would carry me through this difficult time.

The next three infusions were Taxol. That medicine targeted breast cancer cells and would not allow my hair to grow. By this time, a reoccurring pattern was developing. Remember the mention of a "Paw--Paw Day" earlier? Well, every time we headed to Memphis for a treatment the sky would be bright blue and cloudless. It began to dawn on me that every treatment day was a Paw-Paw Day. Now this was unusual because of the time of year. It was another confirmation that God was in control of this wild ride. No matter what you are facing, don't become so distracted that you miss the little miracles that happen daily.

Mixed with the three Taxol treatments was Herceptin. If a patient is diagnosed with HER2 positive cancer, extra treatments are necessary. Herceptin received FDA approval in September 1998. Previously, HER2 positive breast cancer was very difficult to treat. With the development of Herceptin, this type of cancer has become better controlled. I had a total of 17 of these treatments. Most people have never heard of HER2 (Human Epidermal growth factor Receptor 2). It is a protein in the body that causes cells to rapidly reproduce and repair themselves, therefore, making my cancer more aggressive. This is another confirmation that reading and studying about your type of cancer is critical to your recovery. March 14, 2007 marked the end of my treatment journey. That day also marked nine years of marriage for Bob and me. We never want to forget how long it has been since that leg of the journey was completed.

I remember a funny story that involved my port and the access tubing. Bob and I were sitting in the crowded waiting room and I was eagerly awaiting my turn to see the doctor. Becoming bored, I began to use the end of the IV tubing like a microphone. Sitting across from us was a man around eighty years old. He said, "Ma'am, your microphone will work better if you will put in an earpiece!"

It was a very special day in March when that port was accessed for the last time to receive medicine into my body. We were at the West Clinic in Memphis, Tennessee. Upon completion of the treatment, the chemo nurse brought me a cluster of balloons and graduation certificate. We stood before about fifty other patients as she announced my completion. Some of those patients were so sick and fighting for their lives, but they cheered for us. As we stood and cried, our hearts were touched deeply by the love and support from others who were suffering. It was a very humbling experience. Next, we were sent out to the prayer walk to ring a large black bell with a chain so big that Bob had to pull it. The clang seemed to scream to the heavens that Kristi Armstrong was finished with cancer treatments. Bob and I grabbed each other and let the floodgates of joy and relief flow down our faces. Some of the volunteers from the clinic came out to sing the "Chemo Graduation Song." It follows the tune to the Oscar Mayer jingle. The words are by Lisa, a registered nurse, at St. Jude Hospital.

Our patients have the cutest
S-M-I-L-E
Our patients have the sweetest
H-E-A-R-T
OH!
We'd love to see you everyday
But now's the time we get to say
Pack up your bags
Get out the door
You don't get chemo anymore!

Our Family

Luke and Kristina Armstrong Dec. 27, 2005

Zack, our bowler

Luke, Tyler and Kristi

Zack and Kristi

**Our daughter-in-law,
Kristina**

Bob and the Boys

Our boys were a wonderful distraction during the difficult months.

Bob, Tyler and Zack

Tyler and Grand-daddy

Luke, Tyler and Bob

Our world was turned upside-down but Tyler was a bright spot!

**Before
Breast Cancer**

**During
Breast Cancer**

Which one is Bob?

Hair Today
Gone Tomorrow

A little make-up makes everything better.

Who needs hair when you can get a great look with a hat and scarf?

I'm wiggin'

**Even when upon their head
They wear another's hair . . .**

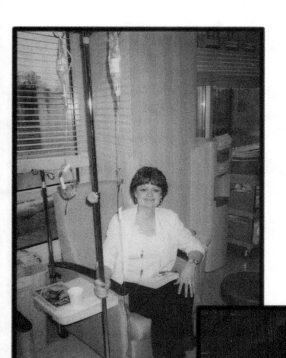

Last of 20 treatments!

If you use your IV for a microphone, be sure to use the ear piece!

Graduation Day!

Bob and Kristi

Ringing the bell! Treatments are over!

My chemo nurse, Cindy Inman

My parents, Lonnie and Bonnie Godwin

**Triumph
Gina Holland
Bro. Allen Guyer
Kristi Armstrong**

A Paw-Paw Day

**Maw Maw Pearl Rich, Kristi, and
Paw Paw Chester Rich**

Bob and his mother, Mama Cile.

An optimist sees this as the perfect opportunity to get a new deck.

Our pastor, Dr. Jerry Spencer and his
wife, Sue were instrumental in the
publication of this book. We thank
them for the insight and help. We
appreciate Dr. Jerry's writings.

Mrs. Kris Smith blessed us with her
writings and editing of the book. We
appreciate her contribution to this work.

My Sunday School Class

Back Row (L to R): Debbie Gannon, Kim Godwin, Sherrie Gray (my encourager), Kris Smith, Kathy Gravett, Mitzi Harris, Melody Scott, Deonne Ewoldt, and Leann Glover.
Front Row (L to R): Marilyn Alexander, Leigh Anne Roberts, Laurie Willoughby, Kristi Armstrong, Kristy Guyer (my teacher) and Gina Rainey.

My Journal

This is the journal I kept during my cancer journey. It was given to me exactly three years before my mastectomy. Notice that the woman is on the bridge alone. If you have cancer, you have to make the trip. Friends and family will be there for support, but you have to cross the bridge to get to the other side.

Sharon Baptist Church Celebration Choir

In all things give PRAISE!

DVD recording, January 13, 2006. This was three weeks after the mastectomy and four days before chemotherapy.

The Wind Beneath My Wings

To the man who stood by me in the good
and bad, happiness and sorrow.
I Love You Bob, with all my heart.
Tootsie

Chapter Five

Wilderness Wear

Some people call this fight with cancer a journey. Well, if I'm going on a trip, I usually carry a few things. Let me take you on a tour of what was in my suitcase. Emotionally, you need a big dose of faith and trust, faith in the Lord and trust in your doctors. Educate yourself so that you can ask your doctor intelligent questions about your treatment path and don't be afraid of what the answers might be. You can handle things better if you see the big picture. At this time, your body is handling a lot of extra stress, so try to lighten your responsibilities until you get better. Your doctor will help you by mapping out your course through cancer treatment. If you are going to a place never traveled before, it is always important to bring a map. Caring people will give their opinions and advice, so listen and glean the information that helps you. In the end, you have to live with your choices. With breast cancer, many decisions will have to be made. Sometimes, you have a choice of a lumpectomy versus a mastectomy. It is your choice whether or not to take chemotherapy, if necessary, or radiation. In my case, I had a mastectomy followed by chemotherapy with no radiation necessary. Everyone's path takes different turns on this road to recovery. While juggling your own emotions, you must also work toward encouraging your family and close friends. Be honest about your feelings and this will benefit them.

At different times in our lives we face wilderness experiences. If we check in with the wilderness expert in the Bible, Moses, we find his attire to be that of a lowly sheep herder. Oh, to be so fortunate. The breast cancer wilderness dress code is of a slightly different style. Yes, there are head pieces and I'm sure that Moses' head got hot, but he was in the desert. Alright, back up. Cancer treatment can cause hair loss, baldness, and conditions that are not in your normal life experience. Have you ever worn a mop on your head? That was my first experience with a wig. Hats and scarves are another fun adventure. Be creative with your look. At this time, things are changing fast and your self-esteem can take a hard blow. Losing your hair, eyebrows, or eyelashes can make you self-conscious. I used to have to draw my eyebrows on with a pencil. Sometimes, if it was a hot day, part of the line would melt off. What a joy to see your reflection and discover that you only have one and a half of your brows. Laugh about it. It is a lot better than crying.

Another drastic change in life is the missing body part. Accommodating this new body of mine was tricky. Keeping things balanced in the front was challenging. When I was healed enough from the mastectomy, I made a trip to the local medical supply office to get a prosthesis. My self image took a bashing during these adjustments. It took a little work to keep things in perspective. We were planning a trip to the beach in June, so I knew that I would need something special. Well, I was fitted for a water-proof prosthesis. I was worried about it falling out in the water or on the sand. So, if this did happen, we had a plan. Bob and Zack were to step over it and declare, "That is the funniest looking jellyfish that I have ever seen!"

Wearing a prosthesis is sometimes uncomfortable. Yes, it is a big change from having your natural breast to using a prosthesis. But, being alive means more than being symmetrical. Bob has a little signal he gives me if I get a little crooked. He even made me a necklace with a small level on it. His humor is a delight! I became very inventive on ways to help my chest appearance. There are many great products on the market at any medical supply company. Even with that, however, there are still needs for your new body. Work at it. See it as an adventure instead of a burden. Tip: There are ways to still feel like the woman God created you to be. That is all I am going to say about that subject. Let your imagination be your guide!

Bob and I are always looking for a reason to have a party. Coming out of the wilderness of cancer was a golden opportunity to celebrate. My sister-in-law, Karen, hosted a "chemo is over" party at their home. The family got together and surprised me with tear jerking gifts. They each wrote a message of thanksgiving for the completion in a special journal. The cake had my Psalm 118:17 scripture in bold letters. "I shall not die, but live, and declare the works of the Lord." It was time to start living and declaring the works of God. Yes, this path is hard but loving people make the journey smoother.

I am usually a few minutes late for

Sunday school but on March 18th, the Sunday following my last treatment, I was actually on time. To my dismay, Bob seemed to be dragging his feet. I found out later that it was on purpose. I went rushing into my classroom for a great shock. There was a cake shaped like a shirt but it was anatomically correct for my body. Grapefruits sliced in halves with cherries on top served as memorials to my lost body part. You may think this was crazy but actually, it was very therapeutic. Some of the women even wore bras on the outside of their clothes with the left side cut out. Yes, the windows were securely covered with newspapers. I will never forget the outpouring of love and support. Mrs. Kris Smith, who is known for her creative writings, blessed me with my own personalized poem.

A Special Gift

Some people have a special gift,
A way to make folks smile;
Even when the path they're on,

Presents them with a trial.

Yes, some folks search for laughter,
And find that it is there;
Even when upon their head,
They wear another's hair!

And even when a painted brow,
Like Frosty, melts away;
One still can hear a laugh break out,
Their humor just won't sway.

They'll greet you with a smile,
They're glad to give a hug,
But don't be too surprised if then,
They give themselves a tug.

For things might need adjusting,
To make them parallel;
A level might be needed,
So parts won't go pell-mell!

If laughter is a medicine,
Then these folks may OD;
For even when their body's weak,
Their spirit goes, "tee-hee!"

Determined to be positive,
And sure that God knows best;

Their worries are all swept away,
As in His arms they rest.

Yes, some folks have a special gift,
And you, dear child, are one;
You've faced your trial with style and
grace,
By God's strength you have won!

While cancer cells were weakening,
Your faith was gaining strength;
You learned that for His precious child,
Your God would span great lengths.

So thank you for the witty way,
In which you faced this test;
And for each laugh you left to show,
The pathway of the blest!

May each of us remember when,
Life deals to us a blow;
That if we don't forget to laugh,
In us God's strength will show!

- Kristine Smith, March 18, 2007

Mrs. Kris Smith is the principal of Savannah Christian Academy, a ministry of Sharon Baptist Church. In the next chapter, we asked her to share her view of our cancer journey.

From the Outside, Looking In

If you're like me, the only thing worse than receiving bad news for yourself is receiving bad news about someone you know and love. You feel physically sick as you wonder what emotions they are feeling and what thoughts they are thinking. You do a quick self-assessment and ask yourself, what if it were me? What would I do? How would I act? Would I want others to ask me how I was doing, or would I want them to act like everything was okay? Would I grow tired of people's worried expressions or would I find comfort in their sympathetic glances? When you have not experienced a serious illness or have not walked beside a loved one who has, your fear of saying the wrong thing can too often keep you from saying anything at all. This could have been the case with Kristi, but it wasn't. My fears of putting my foot in my mouth around Kristi were unfounded, for, more often than not, Kristi was too busy pulling her foot out of her own mouth to be able to say anything to me!

When I heard that Kristi Armstrong had cancer, I remember feeling two emotions. First, I was surprised. Kristi has always been so full of life and so energetic that it was hard to imagine anything affecting her, especially something as serious as cancer. Secondly, I was curious. How would this fellow Sunday school classmate, this singer extraordinaire, this outspoken, in-your-face believer in Jesus Christ deal with such a diagnosis? Would she walk by faith, or would she falter by the flesh? Not only would time answer these questions, but so too would Kristi, and Bob, and Zack, and everyone else who knows this amazing woman!

Kristi's experience with cancer taught

her many lessons. This book is a compilation of much of the knowledge and wisdom that God revealed to her. But, as I've come to learn, God rarely makes a direct hit without allowing an effective "splash" to fall upon those who are standing near His target. I know this is true in Kristi's case for I have definitely had some knowledge, and I pray some wisdom as well, splashed on me. As a result of Kristi's experience with cancer I have learned that:

1. Cancer may attack the white-blood cells but it is powerless against the 'saved by grace' blood cells.
2. Cancer may weaken the body, but it can also strengthen the spirit.
3. Cancer may take away one's hair, but it can never take away one's crown.
4. Cancer may unleash cries of anguish, but it cannot bridle tears of joy.
5. Cancer may mar the symmetry of one's body, but it can restore the shape of one's soul.

Yes, I've learned a lot through Kristi Armstrong's experience with cancer. I've learned that watching a fellow Christian walk by faith creates in me a resolve to do the same. I see, from the outside looking in, that how one deals with the trials in her own life greatly affects how others will walk when a similar experience comes their way. And, while God speaks directly to us through His Word, He also speaks to us through His children. When we submit ourselves to His will and to His way, His image is so transparent in us that others cannot help but to see it, and then cannot help but to desire it. When I look at Kristi, I see double; her face on the outside, with my Father's face shining through from the inside.

In Kristi Armstrong I have seen a woman who not only accepted her diagnosis of cancer, but who also embraced it. Through her illness and through her recovery, she has shown that, by God's grace, you can live, love, laugh, and lean. What a beautiful witness she has been to me and to everyone in our church family. Kristi's openness and honesty during her illness not only gave us a peek into the physical world of cancer, but it also gave us a view into the spiritual world of faith.

I pray that you, the reader, will be able to learn from Kristi's example as I have. I pray that you will learn to lean upon God and to embrace the plan He has for your life. And, I pray that you will not allow the enemy to build up walls between you and the ones you love. Share with them, cry with them, laugh with them, and above all, pray with them! You are still the same person you were before your diagnosis, and so are they!

Be merciful to me, O God, be merciful to me! For my soul trusts in You; And in the shadow of Your wings I will make my refuge, Until these calamities have passed by.

(Psalm 57:1)

Chapter Seven

Fear or Faith

I received Christ as my Savior at the age of seven. He has guided me through many trials in life. When I was twelve years old, my family lost everything in a house fire. I watched my mom and dad as they "walked by faith and not by sight". God performed miracle after miracle as we rebuilt our lives. We lost our house but we still had our home. I believe that watching my parents deal with this hard knock helped prepare me for my fight with breast cancer. I cannot tell you that I understand why I have had to endure cancer, but I can say that God has had a plan for me throughout the entire experience. Much prayer and Bible study has helped me keep things in perspective.

I sing in a trio with Bro. Allen Guyer, our Minister of Worship, and Gina Holland, a close friend and fellow choir member. We had a singing engagement booked just two days after my cancer diagnosis. Bro. Allen called to see if I wanted him to cancel. I told him that we should still go and fulfill our obligation. We went to Parsons, Tennessee and sang out with all our hearts. Near the end of the program, Bro. Allen asked if I would like to share. I started like this. Thursday, I received the phone call that you never want to get. "Yes, Mrs. Armstrong, it is cancer." Everything went quiet. I remember the silence being deafening. The next song up was my solo for "Even in the Valley" written by Rebecca Peck. It speaks of God carrying His children through the valley like He promised He would. I told the people there that God would see me through this valley. I will never forget the peace that flooded me at that moment. God was up to something.

The next morning at our home church, Sharon Baptist, I had asked my pastor, Dr. Jerry Spencer, to have special prayer for us. After the prayer, I again sang the song that even in the valley God is good. From that moment on, it seemed as if the words I had sung became a spotlight of conviction. Was I going to trust God or fear cancer? I chose to trust.

Coping with fear is sometimes a daily struggle. Just when you think you have it conquered, another troubling thought crosses your mind. But as I have shared about miracle after miracle, large and small that God performed, it would be a horrible injustice for me to say one thing and think another. When you choose to walk by faith, then walk by faith.

In chapter three of Daniel, Shadrach, Meshach, and Abednego were bound and thrown into a fiery furnace. The circumstances were out of their control. But by faith, they stated in verses 16-18 that the God they served was able to save them from the fiery furnace. But even if He did not save them, they would never worship another god or image of gold. God did save them from the fire. When they emerged, the only things gone were the ropes that bound them. They did not even smell like smoke!

In my walk, I did have to face the fire of cancer but I feel that God miraculously brought me through. I believed that I was healed, but I still had to go through surgery and treatment. In my heart I felt that I could not lead where I had not walked. Now, my prayer is that I can make the way a little clearer and easier for a "Bosom Buddy" who may one day find herself traveling this same path.

I am extremely blessed to have my husband, Bob, with me during each step of this journey. He will never know how much his love, devotion, patience, and support mean to me. God places special people in our lives for difficult situations. I know this to be true of our marriage.

One thing that stands out to me is the value of family and friends. They are your best support group. For five months during the hardest chemo treatments, there was always a card or letter in our mailbox from a friend, family member, or someone who had heard of our troubles. We have them stored in a special box to never forget the love sent from so many sources to keep us encouraged. We send out a big "thank you" to the folks who took the time to write. My Sunday School class would bring our meals the day after each chemo. We are God's hands extended and sometimes those hands need to hold a chicken pot pie.

You need trusted confidants to help you sort through your feelings. Emotions run high during any traumatic life event. Little things that never bothered you will get on your nerves because your nervous system is doing everything it can to cope. Realize that this is normal and that you are not going crazy. I have told Bob countless times that I thought I was losing my mind. Making a plan for treatment and recovery helps to bring clarity to the chaos. Ask your doctor questions when you are unclear or confused about your case.

There are many ways to keep your

heart from fearing your situation. If you try to keep everything to yourself, the load will get too heavy to bear. I am a very talkative person, so one of my therapies has been talking about where I am in my cancer walk. If your personality is different, writing your feelings down will help to vent them, but try to find some outlet of human support to keep your faith strong. Other breast cancer survivors are a marvelous source of insight and guidance. I am a volunteer for the American Cancer Society's Reach to Recovery. In this program, survivors are sent to newly diagnosed persons with pamphlets of information, words of wisdom, and a listening ear. If you are a cancer patient or have any cancer issues, please call 1-800-ACS-2345. You can do a self referral to the American Cancer Society. There are many resources available with ACS, all you need to do is call.

*Chapter Eight*_____

Where Are We Now?

I started my five years of Tamoxifen in April, 2007. Then came the hot flashes. They were so bad that Bob had a T-shirt made for my Mother's Day gift that read:

"My husband says I'm hot and it comes in flashes!" - Cancer Survivor

After permission from my oncologist, I had the port removed on May 25, 2007. In July, Bob carried, Zack, our nephew, Joseph, and me to ride roller coasters at Disneyworld and Universal Studios. It turned into two days of celebrating "getting back into life." Bob says that I got my laugh back at the expense of his hearing.

We were on one of the rides that had a

lot of special effects. At one point, the coaster stopped, went backwards, then came to an abrupt stop. Then, the ceiling burst into flames and we felt intense heat. I asked Bob, "Is it hot in here or am I having a hot flash!" He said, "Is this what it feels like?" "Yes!" I replied. So, if any of you women need a visual aid for your husband, visit Universal Studios.

I received a clean body scan on May 17, 2007. You never realize what the word clean means until it involves your report after cancer. I remember getting the test results from my first normal mammogram after breast cancer. The word "normal" was written in large letters across the top. I put it on the refrigerator because I was so proud to have a medical paper with my name and the word normal together.

After this journey, the normal we knew was now a "new normal." Things are not the same. Never will be. But we embrace change. If we are not changing, we are not growing. Life is like a puzzle but you do not have the box top to see what the finished picture looks like. So, patiently take the pieces as God directs and watch the picture unfold.

Coping with the changes to my body and life is sometimes challenging. One thing I remember is to not lose my sense of humor. Yes, cancer can be life threatening and very serious. But even then, if you truly trust in God, a good sense of humor will help sustain you through the dark days. The surgery and treatment of breast cancer can leave you with what feels like a shell of who you were. Adjustments have to be made with these changes. Self-esteem takes a very hard knock. First, I lost my left breast. Then, I lost all my hair (thankfully, it is back) and gained twenty pounds. Now that will bless you. What I lost on front showed up in the back! I just decided to accept this new body. I am not thinking of reconstruction right now. I went through fifteen months of treatments and of not feeling well. At this time, more surgery is at the bottom of my list of priorities.

If you have hard issues to settle, make a list. Bob calls me the post-it note queen. When something bothers me, I write it down. I note whatever I can do to help the situation and then I make a plan. If the problem is something that is out of my hands, I leave it totally with God. He never makes a mistake. On this path, trust is vital for sanity. I make myself forget the things that I cannot change. This acceptance frees up emotion and brain space for other pressing needs.

Keeping a journal was another good stress reliever. A beautiful brown journal was given to me as a present on December 21, 2002. At the time, I just thought that it was a nice gesture from my friend, Dianah. I started using it to record my cancer walk in November. The surgery date changed two or three times, but finally fell on December 21, 2005. That's right, three years before I even knew I had cancer, God had a friend give me a special blessing. He was letting me know that He was in total control of this situation. The front cover was also significant. A woman was pictured crossing a bridge to the other side of a river. I knew that the Lord was going to take me to the other side of cancer. Looking at the picture, the woman was alone on the bridge. She had to make to journey by herself. That is how it is in many of life's situations. Family and friends would love to help or even take the suffering and pain. But they cannot. Bob wanted to cross the bridge for me. My sister, Angela, prayed for me everyday during treatments. She could not take them for me, but she did the next best thing-she prayed. If you are facing a bridge spanning turbulent waters, just reach up and hold on to God's mighty, strong hand. Then, take the walk to the other side, one step at a time.

God has taught us so much through this situation. "For I know the thoughts that I think toward you," as He stated in Jeremiah 29:11. Another scripture that helped carry us is Psalm 118:17: "I shall not die, but live, And declare the works of the Lord." This little book is dedicated to the promise I made to God the day after my diagnosis, to declare His works. Thank you for reading this book and for allowing me to keep that promise.

In closing, our prayer is that you cried a little, laughed a lot, and learned from our experience with breast cancer. But most of all, we pray that you learned that when you call on Jesus, ALL THINGS ARE POSSIBLE!

One day, we will receive a new body that will never see sickness or death. Until then, pray to the Lord for a clean heart and don't sweat the spare parts.

Conclusion

Do You Know the Giver and Sustainer of Life? The Lord Jesus Christ has promised us in John 10:10: *"My purpose is to give them a rich and satisfying life."*

This abundant life is not possible through any other means in the universe other than a personal faith in Jesus Christ.

DISEASED DNA

The first human couple to inhabit the earth was, of course, Adam and Eve. They chose to disobey God. The debilitating and deadly disease of sin is now in the spiritual DNA of every person who is born. There is only one cure for the disease of sin — That cure is Dr. Jesus.

RECEIVE JESUS NOW

Would you like to receive the Savior

who has so dramatically and wonderfully transformed and sustained Kristi Armstrong? Jesus is only a prayer away. Let us suggest that you pray a prayer like this:

"Dear Jesus, like all other human beings I am 'sin sick.' I do not want to continue to live alienated from God. I want my sins to be forgiven. Right now, Lord Jesus, I want You to know that I am choosing against sin and I invite You to come into my heart."

If you invited Jesus to come into your heart, He has answered your sincere prayer and is living in you. Now you may want to pray this prayer of thanksgiving:

"I love You, Lord. Thank You for being willing to be the everlasting cure for my sin-diseased soul. Lord Jesus Christ, I have given You the control of my life. I am confident that You will Personally sustain me in this life and when I die, You will take me to live with You in Heaven."

A Clean Heart and Spare Parts

...The Journey Continues

Fast forward exactly fourteen years from the mastectomy on December 21, 2005. Bob and I spent our first night in our new home. We moved to his mom and dad's house on December 21, 2018 after a complete remodel. We didn't plan on the date but it just worked out that way. Little did we know that God was placing us on another journey. A few months later, all became clear as the path revealed itself before us. Faith is like film. It has to be developed in the dark. March 6, 2019, we were summoned to the dark room... In December 2018, I began losing weight due to being sick at my stomach multiple times a day. I began to sleep a lot, sometimes up to sixteen hours a day, and by January 2019, my right ear began to have a roaring sound. The best way to describe it is like driving your car with one back window rolled down while on the interstate traveling at seventy miles per hour. Then, every three minutes, a motorcycle would pass going at least ninety miles an hour. This became concerning to us, so I scheduled an appointment with an ENT doctor in Jackson TN. The first available appointment was at the end of March but the office instructed me to call everyday in hopes to move the appointment to an earlier time. There was finally a cancellation that gave me time to see the doctor in February. During the appointment, all symptoms pointed towards meniere's disease. As the doctor was leaving the room, he asked if we would like to have an MRI. We promptly said yes and the test was scheduled for the next week. God didn't promise us an easy passage across the stormy sea of life, just a safe landing. In Mark 4:35 the disciples encountered a storm but Jesus said, "Let us go to the other side." Sometimes Jesus calms the storms in our lives. Other times, He lets the storm rage and calms His child. My first diagnosis with breast cancer was in 2005. In August 2015, Dr. Arnel Pallera, my oncologist at West Cancer Center in Memphis TN, pronounced me cured of triple positive cancer. There was no time to celebrate because my dear sister, Angela, was fighting breast cancer. By November 2015, the cancer had metastasized to her brain. We celebrated her 52nd birthday on November 28 never thinking that she would be in Heaven by December 28th. Proverbs 18:10 "The name of the Lord is a strong tower. The righteous run to it and are safe." In March 2019, as we awaited the results of the MRI, our world began to enter a storm. On March 4, we received a call from Semmes Murphey clinic. The lady said that I needed to come for an appointment to meet with Dr. Jeffery Sorenson for the MRI results the next day. At this time, Bob was president of our Savannah Gideon camp and the annual Pastor's banquet was in three days. I told the lady that I would come the following week. On Tuesday morning, the West Cancer Center called and told me that I needed to go to Semmes Murphey for the MRI results the next morning. I began to explain about the banquet but she kindly interrupted me and said that she needed us to drop everything and be at the clinic the next morning at 9:30am. We agreed to come never thinking of the results being life changing. On the morning of March 6, 2019, we arrived for the appointment with Dr. Sorenson. The MRI revealed cancer on the right side of the brain and at the base of the spine. The doctor said that I needed to be in the hospital for a few days for more tests. Again, I told him that we could next week. He politely said, "Your room is being prepared right now at Methodist University Hospital." There are times in life that we lose total control of everything. That is when total confidence and trust in God has to be relied on to carry us through the days. We checked in at the hospital without any clothes or supplies. I was scheduled to start tests at 4am the next morning, so Bob planned to go home and pack for us. Early the next morning, Bob left when I was taken for tests and my parents left Savannah to be at the hospital when I was back at the room. I returned to the room at 8am then Mom and Dad arrived around 8:15. As we were talking, an oncologist came to the room. He had news to give me from the tests. He proceeded to tell us that I had six months to live, but he would get me another month and a half with chemotherapy. Now remember, my family had said good-bye for now to my sister a little over three years ago. I closed my eyes and tried to absorb the news as the doctor was leaving the room. It was two months later that we learned that Daddy followed him. Anyone who knows our Daddy knows that he has never been afraid to share his faith in Jesus. If that doctor didn't know about Jesus, he does now. We were dismissed from the hospital on March 9th with a diagnosis of brain and spine cancer with the spinal fluid being cloudy with the presence of HER2 cancer cells. Dr. Pallera, my oncologist for the past fourteen years, was on vacation, so I was told that I would be contacted soon. Time out for a story: You can go to YouTube to learn about the buffalo and cow on the prairie. When a storm comes over the mountains, the buffalo will run toward the storm. Although he is in the storm, he continues until he finally runs through the storm.

The cow turns and walks with the storm, so she is in it for a longer time. On Monday morning after being in the hospital, Bob and I decided to be the buffalo. And now a note from Bob: The last couple of months of 2018 and all of 2019 were a blur. Remodeling my parents 50 year old house was fun but challenging. (I really liked the demolition part) When the moving began, Kristi had started showing some signs of illness. We first thought it was due to the stress of downsizing because our living space was cut to about a third of what we were accustomed to so we started giving things to our boys. After about twenty truck loads, our daughters-in-law almost got to the point of forbidding our visits if we had anything in the back of the truck. Kristi earned her "Wife of the Year" award when she let me build a shop bigger than the house. (The logic behind that statement will be clarified a little later) Kristi has discussed the journey from diagnosis to treatment, etc. After the radiation was completed and the chemo started, Kristi went through a period of sleeping up to sixteen hours a day. The treatment was brutal and obviously the cancer was taking a major toll on her. We had the conversation again of how I would be if she was not here. I don't like discussing that, but it did need to be considered. Thankfully, God gave us peace about the situation.

Even if it did not turn out like we wanted, God is still in control. He says we will know as we are known in Heaven, so I would see her again sooner and later. Kristi has been an excellent Guinea Pig for these treatments. Since West Cancer Center had never put Herceptin straight to the brain through the ommaya reservoir, they had a learning curve. The first treatment caused her to be more violently ill than I had ever seen. The nurses were amazed to see her show up for the second treatment. The tweaking of the treatments have allowed the most recent ones to be more tolerable. From a caregiver standpoint, this last year has been challenging. My concern for Kristi has been my primary focus. Our age difference of eighteen years is a blessing. I am technically a retired part time employee of Woodmen Life. I do not have the stress of having to work forty hours a week. Like fifteen years ago, we have Woodmen members all over the country praying for us. These along with the countless number of people in our town, county, state and all over are praying too. These prayers have absolutely sustained us and we pray that these prayer warriors will be abundantly blessed with a strengthening of their faith. Caregivers need some encouragement too. It is nice to hear someone ask how I am doing. Fortunately, we have a great network of family and extended family who give us an incredible amount of support. Trust in God is by far the most important aspect of dealing with life altering events. If you are in this or a similar situation, please be sure of your relationship with Jesus Christ. Be confident of your relationship with Him even if you are not in one of these situations. Over the years, I have dealt with stress through what I call 'pittling.' During times of loss, I have built clubhouses, side sheds, and tractor sheds. I have a few things to show for my 'stress work'. This time I was able to do some work in the shop I spoke of earlier. During some of Kristi's long naps, I would spend some time in the shop. I could check on her and still get some work done. It was a nice and necessary distraction to be able to do some wiring, wall building, and organizing. Through this, I learned at least one very valuable lesson. A sixty nine year old man should not reach beyond a comfortable limit when almost to the top of an eight foot step ladder. It is amazing how much skin you can lose from the inside of your arm and down your side when you fall with your arm on one side of a sheet of OSB and your ribs are on the other side. I waited several days before I showed Kristi the damage. Back to Kristi: On March 11, 2019, Bob and I traveled to the West Cancer Center in Corinth, Mississippi, a branch office of the West Cancer Center in Memphis. In 2006 and 2007, I received many of my treatments at this location. My nurse, Mrs. Jeri Simpson, was still working there so we still knew a lot of the staff at this location. We felt comfortable showing up without an appointment. Bob and I went to the reception desk and told the receptionist that I had been diagnosed with brain and spine cancer the week before and Dr. Pallera in Memphis was on vacation. I told her that we had to get some kind of treatment started and she agreed. She went to talk to the doctor over radiation, Dr. Micah Monaghan, and he came to speak with us. He said that he would give Dr. Pallera a call to ask if there were any orders for treatment. After a while, Dr. Monaghan returned with orders for ten days of brain radiation. Being like the buffalo on the prairie was getting treatment started. The next day, we returned to have my radiation mask made and the schedule for ten treatments. On the first treatment, I was in the radiation room and Bob was in the waiting room feeling rough emotions. Dr. Monaghan and his nurse had a prayer for Bob to have strength for the days we were facing. God always supplies everything we need exactly when we need it. Bro. Larry Littlefield, our sister-in-law Karen's Dad, had recently had brain radiation for a benign brain tumor so I gave him a call. He was so kind to share his experience with me so I would know what to expect. When flashing lights, securing my head to the table with the mask, and other things occurred, I was prepared because he had shared his story with me. What is your story? I believe that we are to help others by sharing the good and bad to prepare people for what lies ahead of them on their journey. We had an appointment in Memphis with Dr. Pallera and at his request, we changed to Dr. Lee Shcwartzberg because he specialized in the treatment that was needed for me. We agreed for the change and were so blessed that Cindy Inman, my nurse from the first time through cancer, was working with Dr. Schwartzberg. This was a difficult season of life but we felt peace in the fact that God was in control. An ommaya reservoir was placed in my head by surgery to receive chemotherapy directly to the brain. At this time, I have received twelve treatments and the next one is in May. When I was diagnosed, the spinal fluid was cloudy with cancer cells, but praise God, the fluid is now clear even on a microscopic level. I still have a roaring sound in my right ear, but it is much better than last year. When studying the membrane that surrounds the brain and spine, we learned that it is surrounded by a blood barrier that has three parts- God the Father, God the Son, and God the

Holy Spirit. Our creator thought of everything. The first time we went through cancer, Tyler, our first grandson and Luke's oldest, was just two years old. Ironically, Zack's son, Carson, was two years old when we received this new diagnosis. Luke and Kristina are blessed now with a fifteen year old, Tyler, and an eight year old, Lilian. Zack and Miranda are blessed with two year old Carson and newborn, Camden. We thank the Lord for blessing our family so abundantly. On March 6, 2020, I was invited to give my testimony to Cornerstone Baptist Church. The Wednesday morning prayer group had lifted me in prayer for the past year. It was a special night that marked my one year from the recurrence. We had a special prayer by Brenda Spears to stop and say thank you to our Heavenly Father for life and answered prayers. On Sunday, March 8th, I was to give testimony to the youth at Calvary Baptist Church. My mom had invited me the month before to share with their young people. During the worship service, my brother Patrick, who is the pastor, asked if I would speak to the congregation instead of just the youth. I agreed and Mom took the kids twelve and under to children's church. At the close, Patrick gave an invitation, and thanks to the Lord, two young men accepted Christ. That gives the cancer journey a great purpose. Our lives should direct people to Christ. Dad wrote a song years ago that is still true today: He's my storehouse of love and my fortress When my strength is gone He carries me through When my pathway is dark He's there to guide me Whatever I need in this life I go to Jesus Whatever you need, you can go to Jesus. He will never let you down. Psalm 46:10 "Be still and know that I am God." In closing, I want to share a thought about the ten lepers in Luke 17. Jesus sent them to see the priest and they were cleansed as they went. Now, ten lepers received the miracle, but only one returned to say thank you. How many times have we prayed and asked God for various things? Take some time in prayer to thank God for anything that comes to mind. When I was first diagnosed with the recurrence, our niece, Kaylin, made a powerful statement. She was talking to her mom, Karen, and said, "He'll do it again." She didn't know that is the title of one of my favorite songs by Karen Wheaton. As for Bob and me, we will continue to trust God with, well, everything. Join us. I promise you will not be disappointed. Hebrews 13:8 "Jesus is the same, yesterday and forever."

Bob and Kristi

**Luke, Kristina,
Tyler & Lillian**

**Zach, Miranda,
Carson & Camden**